This
Naure Storybook
belongs to:

_____

_____

To Connie and Roscoe Blanchard, and Isobel Shooter – N.D.
To Sam and Chloe – M.F.

First published 2007 by Walker Books Ltd, 87 Vauxhall Walk, London SE11 5HJ

This edition published 2016

2 4 6 8 10 9 7 5 3 1

Text © 2007 Nicola Davies   Illustrations © 2007 Michael Foreman

The right of Nicola Davies and Michael Foreman to be identified as author and illustrator respectively of this work
has been asserted by them in accordance with the Copyright, Designs and Patents Act 1988

This book has been typeset in Garamond Ludlow

Printed in China

British Library Cataloguing in Publication Data: a catalogue record for this book is available from the British Library

ISBN 978-1-4063-6544-3

www.walker.co.uk

WHITE OWL, BARN OWL

Nicola Davies

illustrated by Michael Foreman

WALKER BOOKS
AND SUBSIDIARIES
LONDON • BOSTON • SYDNEY • AUCKLAND

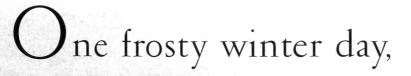

One frosty winter day,

I helped my grandpa make a big wooden box.

"What's it for, Grandpa?"

"It's for the barn owls to nest in," he said.

"What barn owls?" I asked.

But Grandpa just smiled.

"Wait and see," he said.

We carried the box across
the tussocky field.

Barn owls like to nest
in old farm buildings or hollow
tree trunks. Where there aren't any,
they will use a nest-box instead.

7

Grandpa put it high in
the old oak tree.

"How do you know there are
barn owls here?" I asked.

"I've seen one sitting on that
branch at night," Grandpa said.

"Look, it's left something behind..."
Under the branch was a pile of
little sausage-shaped blobs. They
looked like dried poos, but
Grandpa said they were pellets.

Barn owl pellet,
real size.

8

Barn owls have
favourite perches
that they come back to
again and again.

"The owls spit them out," Grandpa said,

"to get rid of the fur and bones they can't eat."

He pulled a pellet to bits and showed me

the tiny bones and skulls inside.

Owls swallow their prey
whole and don't have teeth to chew with.
That's why they need to spit out the bones and fur.

"Will the owl come to our box tonight?"

"Maybe," said Grandpa, "maybe not. Owls are wild

birds, you can't be sure what they'll do."

10

In winter, barn owls have to fly miles every night to find enough food, so they can be hard to spot.

When the sun went down, we kept a lookout
just in case ... but we didn't see anything.
"We'll have to be patient," said Grandpa.

We were patient
lots of times!

I thought we'd
never see an owl.

And then, one spring night,

just as the sky went pink,

a pale face looked out

of our box...

An owl!

A white owl!

A barn owl!

14

In spring and summer,
owls stay quite close
to their nests.

And then Grandpa did a strange thing. He put his hand over his mouth and made a loud squeaky sound.

Straight away the owl took off and flew towards us. "He thinks I'm a vole or mouse in the grass," Grandpa whispered. "He's coming to see if he can catch his dinner!"

I just held my breath. The owl's whiteness gleamed and its face was like a pearly heart.

A barn owl's huge eyes can see when it's too dark for human eyes to work. The heart-shaped ruff around its face helps to guide sound to its super-sharp ears — just holes under the feathers on its head.

Under their feathers,
owls are quite slim.
Their bones are hollow
to keep their bodies
light and make
flying easy.

The owl came closer and closer, then landed in the tree – right by our hiding place! It was so light, it hardly bent the twig it perched on.

I could see the tiny ruff of feathers round its face, like stiff lace. I could see the speckled browns on its back. I could see the shine of its big dark eyes. I could have reached out to touch its velvety softness.

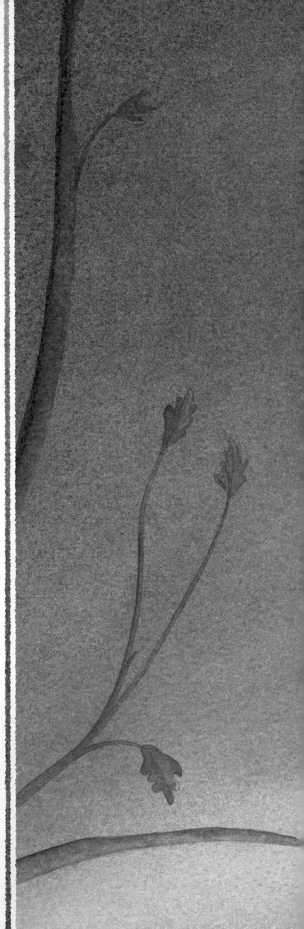

And then it raised its wings

like an angel and took off.

It was so quiet, all I heard

was my own heart beating.

Owl wing feathers are especially
soft so they can move through the air
silently and fly up to their prey
without being heard.

Barn owls catch their prey
by pouncing with their long legs
and needle-sharp talons.

The owl flew back and forth over the field. Then another owl came to join it. "That's its mate," Grandpa whispered.

One owl dropped to the ground and came up again. "Look! Look, Grandpa! It's caught something!" I said.

The owl flew straight to the box and went inside.

"*Hissssss, snorrre, twitter, twitter, hisss. Snoorrrrreeee.*"

The weirdest noises came from Grandpa's box.

Barn owls lay up to six eggs that hatch one after another.
The first chicks to hatch are the biggest and the
last to hatch are the smallest.

"They've got a family!" Grandpa whispered.

"That's the baby owls squabbling over their dinner."

I held Grandpa's hand and we walked home as the moon came up. "Will the barn owls always nest in our box now, Grandpa?" I said. Grandpa smiled. "You know," he said. "I think they might."

Barn owls will come back to the same nest-site year after year if it stays safe and there is enough to eat.

A NEST-BOX NOTE

On modern farms the open grassland where barn owls like to hunt is often ploughed up, and old trees and barns where they can nest are taken down. So barn owls have become rarer. One way to help bring them back is to put up nest-boxes.

The barn owl nest-box in this book is very sturdy and weatherproof because it's outside in a tree, but nest-boxes inside barns, protected from wind and rain, can be very simple: just an old crate will do! The important things for all nest-boxes are that they should be high up (3–5 metres) to be safer from

predators and people, and should have nothing in the way of the entrance, so the owls can fly right in.

You can get information about how to make a nest-box and where to put it from your local wildlife protection organizations. It sometimes takes a while for owls to use a new nest-box, but be patient and you could have a barn owl family in your box!

INDEX

Look up the pages to find out about all these barn owl things.
Don't forget to look at both kinds of word — this kind *and* this kind*.*

Note to Parents

Sharing books with children is one of the best ways to help them learn. And it's one of the best ways they learn to read, too.

Nature Storybooks are beautifully illustrated, award-winning information picture books whose focus on animals has a strong appeal for children. They can be read as stories, revisited and enjoyed again and again, inviting children to become excited about a subject, to think and discover, and to want to find out more.

Each book is an adventure into the real world that broadens children's experience and develops their curiosity and understanding — and that's the best kind of learning there is.

Note to Teachers

Nature Storybooks provide memorable reading experiences for children in Key Stages 1 and 2 (Years 1–4), and also offer many learning opportunities for exploring a topic through words and pictures.

By working with the stories, either individually or together, children can respond to the animal world through a variety of activities, including drawing and painting, role play, talking and writing.

The books provide a rich starting-point for further research and for developing children's knowledge of information genres.

Nature Storybooks support the literacy curriculum in a variety of ways, providing:

- a focus for a whole class topic
- high-quality texts for guided reading
- a resource for the class read-aloud programme
- information texts for the class and school library for developing children's individual reading interests

Find more information on how to use Nature Storybooks in the classroom at
www.walker.co.uk/naturestorybooks

Nature Storybooks support KS 1–2 English and KS 1–2 Science